Chefs' Special

Gujarati Kitchen

Gujarati Kitchen

Vijaylakshmi Baig

Lustre Press
Roli Books

Acknowledgements

My interest in Gujarati food came from my lifetime fascination for food that has also made me a cookery teacher. I have always tried to taste and cook the food of whichever region of India or the world that I have had the opportunity to visit. A very dear cousin in Surat was the occasion for many visits to Gujarat over the past eight years. Cooking for a three-day food festival at one of Surat's 5-Star hotels was a part of these visits. I must confess that I did not initially think too much of this cuisine, but closer exposure taught me that it had a great deal to recommend. To write this book and to really appreciate the cuisine, a normally hardcore non-vegetarian like me, became a vegetarian.

I would like to especially thank Mrs Uma Singh of Farsaan Restaurant in Delhi, for her unstinting help and guidance. She let us photograph food from her Gujarati restaurant. My friend, Asha Mohan, helped me with her Gujarati drapes and utensils. A reputed cook of Surat, Poornima Vantani, sent me some of her favourite Surati recipes.

Dedication

To my husband, Murad Ali Baig, who has constantly helped me in whatever I did.

Flavours of Gujarat

Gujarat, India's western-most region, has for many centuries been the centre of commerce and contact between India and countries beyond the Arabian Sea. Though Gujaratis were exposed to numerous foreign influences, they retained an innate conservatism and pride in their own traditions. The influence of Jainism also contributed to making for a vegetarian tradition that avoided root vegetables such as onions, garlic, beetroot, and carrots.

The evolution of food is linked to history and geography. Gujarati food varies according to different climates. Khatiawar is a dry region where fresh vegetables are rare, but is rich in dairy produce and pickles. Central Gujarat is more agrarian. *Dhokla* (steamed savoury cakes) and *thepla* (thin fried chapatis made of wheat and gram four), the best-known Gujarati fare, come from there because of the variety of vegetables grown there.

Surat was the main Mughal port on the west coast and was exposed to the Persians, Arabs, and Europeans as well as to the exporters from the pepper route of the south, textile producers of the west and buyers of horses from the north. So Surat food is quite different, even though the dish names may be the same. The people from Surat use garlic unlike other Gujaratis. Surati cuisine is fabled and it is said: *Surat nu jaman, ane Kashi nu maran* (Heaven is to taste the food of Surat, and to die in Kashi).

Surat is also known for its *baghar* tradition, which is the tempering of foods with ghee and spices at the end of food preparation. It imparts a distinctive flavour. Gujarati food is always simple and can be prepared quickly with little oil and spices. It tends to use a lot of asafoetida to aid digestion.

For those who find Gujarati food too sweet, the sugar can be cut down up to one-third the quantity prescribed in the recipes. Most Gujaratis are passionate about their food regardless of their social or economic status. Few people realise that *khichdi* was originally a Gujarati dish, brought to Delhi by Prince Khurram, the then Governor of Gujarat before he became emperor Shah Jehan. *Khandvi* (gram flour rolls) was also mentioned in a manuscript of Shah Jehan's time and was called *nemat* during the early seventeenth century.

A traditional Gujarati meal starts with *chaach* (buttermilk tempered with mustard seeds), followed by a *thali* comprising rice, *thepla*, two kinds of vegetables, two kinds of *farsaans*, pickles, chutney, *pappad*, and sweets. *Farsaans* are snacks that are prepared in every Gujarati home. There are numerous snacks to choose from and each household takes pride in its own delicacies. There are several types of *farsaans*. Some are fried and can be kept longer while others are steamed like the *dhokla* and *khandvi*. Then there are the *moothia* made of just gram flour or vegetables. Sweets are served along with the meal and not separately. Many snacks are eaten during the day but at night the meals are usually light. *Thepla*, *bajra rotlo*, *kadhi*, and *khichdi* are eaten at night.

Gujarati cuisine is not difficult to cook as long as you are willing and not afraid to experiment.

Aam Ka Panna
Raw mango appetiser

Preparation time: 10 min.
Cooking time: 30 min.
Serves: 6

Ingredients:

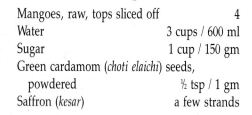

Mangoes, raw, tops sliced off	4
Water	3 cups / 600 ml
Sugar	1 cup / 150 gm
Green cardamom (*choti elaichi*) seeds, powdered	½ tsp / 1 gm
Saffron (*kesar*)	a few strands

Method:

1. Boil the mangoes until tender and pulpy.
2. Peel the skins and scrape off the pulp from the seeds. Discard the seeds.
3. Mix the pulp with the water and strain the mixture.
4. Add the sugar, green cardamom powder, and saffron. Mix well.
5. Serve chilled in individual glasses.

Variation: *If you do not want a sweet preparation then substitute saffron, green cardamom powder and sugar with roasted, ground cumin seeds and salt.*

(Photograph on facing page, left)

Chaach
Buttermilk tempered with mustard seeds

Preparation time: 15 min.
Cooking time: 1 min.
Serves: 3-4

Beverages

Ingredients:

Yoghurt (*dahi*)	1 cup / 180 gm
Cumin (*jeera*) powder, roasted	½ tsp / ¾ gm
Green chilli, small	1
Ginger (*adrak*), ¼" piece	1
Black salt (*kala namak*) to taste	
Salt to taste	
For the tempering:	
Vegetable oil	1 tsp / 5 ml
Mustard seeds (*rai*)	¼ tsp / ¾ gm
Green coriander (*hara dhaniya*), chopped	1 tbsp / 4 gm
Mint (*pudina*) leaves, chopped	1 tbsp / 4 gm

Method:

1. Blend the yoghurt, cumin powder, green chilli, ginger, black salt, and salt for a few seconds.
2. Add 2 cups of water and blend once again. Pour into individual glasses.
3. **For the tempering**, heat the oil in a pan; add the mustard seeds. When they splutter, remove the pan from the heat and pour a little in each glass.
4. Serve chilled, garnished with green coriander and mint leaves.

(Photograph on page 9, right)

Baaflo
A refreshing drink made of raw mangoes

Preparation time: 5 min.
Cooking time: 15 min.
Serves: 4

Ingredients:

Mangoes, raw	250 gm
Water	2 cups / 400 ml
Sugar	4 tbsp / 80 gm
Cumin (*jeera*) powder	1½ tsp / 2¼ gm
Salt to taste	

Method:

1. Roast the mangoes in an open fire. Alternately, pressure cook the mangoes on a high flame with the water. Remove from heat after 2 whistles.
2. When cool enough to handle, peel the mangoes, scrape all the pulp from the seeds. Discard the seeds. Retain the liquid and the pulp.
3. Blend the pulp and the liquid till smooth. Add the sugar, cumin powder, and salt.
4. Stir till the sugar dissolves completely.
5. Pour into individual glasses and serve chilled.

Khandvi
Gram flour rolls

Preparation time: 15 min.
Cooking time: 20 min.
Serves: 6

Ingredients:

Gram flour (*besan*)	2½ cups / 250 gm
Green chillies	4
Ginger (*adrak*), 1" piece	1
Buttermilk (*chaach*), thick	2 cups / 400 ml
Water	2 cups / 400 ml
Turmeric (*haldi*) powder	½ tsp / 1 gm
Salt to taste	

For the tempering:

Vegetable oil	1 tbsp / 15 ml
Mustard seeds (*rai*)	1 tsp / 3 gm
Dry red chillies (*sookhi lal mirch*), cut	2
Asafoetida (*hing*)	a pinch
Curry leaves (*kadhi patta*)	7-8
Coconut (*nariyal*), grated	¼
Green coriander (*hara dhaniya*), chopped	1 cup / 25 gm
Green chillies, slit	5

Method:

1. Grind the green chillies and ginger with a little water to a smooth paste.
2. Mix the buttermilk, gram flour, and water together. Add the turmeric powder, salt, and the chilli-ginger paste. Mix to make a smooth batter.
3. Cook the batter in a pan on a medium flame till a thick paste-like consistency is obtained. Remove the pan from the flame.
4. Grease the reverse side of 2 stainless steel flat plates and spread the mixture as thinly as possible.

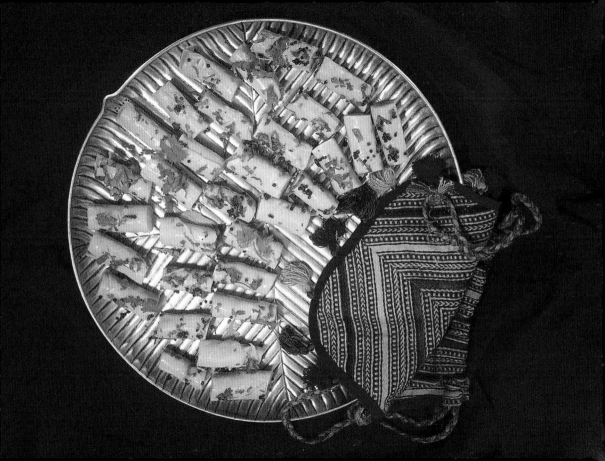

5. While it is still warm, make 1" wide strips with a sharp knife on the spread mixture. When cool, gently roll each strip to resemble small swiss rolls. Arrange the rolls on a serving platter.

6. **For the tempering**, heat the oil in a pan; add the mustard seeds, and when they start spluttering add the dry red chillies and asafoetida. Sauté for a few seconds, remove from heat and pour over the prepared rolls.

7. Garnish with coconut and green coriander; serve either hot or cold.

A Nut in the Freezer
Coconut can be preserved in the freezer for about a week.

Sev
Gram flour savoury

Preparation time: 15 min.
Cooking time: 10 min.
Serves: 6-8

Ingredients:

Gram flour (*besan*)	2½ cups / 250 gm
Vegetable oil	2 tbsp / 30 ml
Carom seeds (*ajwain*)	1 tsp / 1½ gm
Bicarbonate of soda	¼ tsp / 1½ gm
Red chilli powder	1 tsp / 2 gm

Salt to taste
Water as required
Vegetable oil for deep-frying

Method:

1. Mix the oil into the flour and rub until it becomes crumbly.
2. Add all the other ingredients (except water and oil); mix well. Knead with enough water to make a stiff dough.
3. Heat the oil in a wok (*kadhai*); meanwhile grease the insides of a *sev*-making device (or use a noodle maker with a fine mesh to make thinner *sev*).
4. Fill the top container of the device with the dough. Press the dough down through the mesh directly into the hot oil.
5. Separate the *sev* in the oil with a fork to prevent sticking. Fry over a low flame until crisp and pale yellow. Remove with a slotted spoon and drain the excess oil on absorbent kitchen towels.
6. Allow to cool then store in airtight jars.

Note: *Add one third rice flour instead of just gram flour for even more crisper sev.*

Khaman Dhokla

Steamed savoury cakes

Preparation time: 15 min. + overnight
Cooking time: 20 min.
Serves: 6

Ingredients:

Bengal gram (*chana dal*), soaked overnight	1 cup / 160 gm
Green chillies	4
Ginger (*adrak*), 1″ piece	1
Vegetable oil	3 tbsp / 45 ml
Salt to taste	
Asafoetida (*hing*)	¼ tsp / 1 gm
Bicarbonate of soda	¼ tsp / 1½ gm
For the tempering:	
Vegetable oil	1 tbsp / 15 ml
Mustard seeds (*rai*)	½ tsp / 1½ gm
Cumin (*jeera*) seeds	½ tsp / 1 gm

(Photograph on front cover)

Dry red chillies (*sookhi lal mirch*), whole	3-4
Curry leaves (*kadhi patta*)	10
Green coriander (*hara dhaniya*), chopped	½ cup / 12½ gm
Coconut (*nariyal*), grated	¼

Method:

1. Grind the green chillies and ginger to a smooth paste. Keep aside.
2. Grind the Bengal gram coarsely; whisk to incorporate air in it. Keep aside to ferment in a warm place for at least 10 hours or till tiny bubbles appear.
3. Add the oil, salt, asafoetida, bicarbonate of soda,

and green chilli-ginger paste to the Bengal gram paste. Add a little water and whisk the mixture thoroughly once again.

4. Grease a flat stainless steel plate or a baking dish (2" deep). Spread the mixture to a thickness of 1". Steam till it is done. To check if the dish is ready, pierce with a fork. If the fork comes out clean, then the *dhokla* is ready.

5. Allow to cool, then cut into 1-1½" squares.

6. **For the tempering**, heat the oil in a pan; add the mustard seeds, cumin seeds, and dry red chillies. When they start crackling, add the curry leaves and pour over the *dhokla*.

7. Serve garnished with coconut and green coriander.

≈

Yoghurt Sweetly Set
Yoghurt will set faster if a pinch of sugar is added to the milk.

≈

Matri
Crisp flour biscuits flavoured with carom seeds

Preparation time: 15 min.
Cooking time: 15 min.
Serves: 4-6

Ingredients:

Refined flour (*maida*)	1 cup / 100 gm
Ghee	1 tbsp / 15 gm
Salt to taste	
Bicarbonate of soda	2-3 pinches
Carom seeds (*ajwain*)	¼ tsp
Warm water for kneading	
Vegetable oil for deep-frying	

Method:

1. Mix all the ingredients (except water and oil) together. Knead into a pliable dough by adding just enough warm water. Cover the dough and keep aside for 15 minutes.
2. Divide the dough equally into small portions. Roll out each into a 1"-wide, thick disc. Prick the surface with a fork and place over a clean cloth. Similarly, prepare the other portions.
3. Heat the oil in a frying pan; fry the discs, a few at a time, till crisp and golden on both sides. Remove with a slotted spoon and drain the excess oil on absorbent kitchen towels.
4. When cool, store in airtight containers.

Mag Ni Dal Na Bhajiya
Fried green gram dumplings

Preparation time: 4 hrs.
Cooking time: 30 min.
Serves: 6-8

Ingredients:

Split green gram (*dhuli moong dal*), with skin,
    soaked for 4 hours or overnight   500 gm
Green chillies   4
Black peppercorns (*sabut kali mirch*),
    coarsely ground   15
Asafoetida (*hing*)   a pinch
Salt to taste
Vegetable oil for deep-frying

Method:

1. Remove the skin of the green gram by rubbing between your palms and then washing in plenty of water. Drain the excess water.
2. Add the green chillies and blend to a smooth paste without adding any water.
3. Transfer the mixture into a large bowl and then whisk well with your hand, till light and fluffy.
4. Heat the oil in a wok (*kadhai*); gently drop spoonfuls of the mixture and deep-fry on a medium flame for about 3 minutes or until golden brown and crisp. Remove and drain the excess oil. Repeat till all the batter is used up.
5. Serve hot with *kothmir ni chutney* (see p. 82).

Lavingya Paatra
Colocasia leaves rolled in gram flour paste

Preparation time: 25 min.
Cooking time: 10 min.
Serves: 4-5

Ingredients:

Colocasia leaves, cut into 4 pieces — 10
For the paste, mix together till smooth:
Gram flour (*besan*) — 1½ cups / 150 gm
Wholewheat flour (*atta*) — 1 cup / 100 gm
Yoghurt (*dahi*), fresh — 1 cup / 180 gm
Turmeric (*haldi*) powder — 1 tsp / 2 gm
Sugar — 5 tsp / 15 gm
Green coriander (*hara dhaniya*),
  chopped — 2 tbsp / 8 gm
Green chilli-ginger (*adrak*) paste — 1 tsp / 6 gm
Soybean oil — 4 tbsp / 60 ml
For the tempering:
Vegetable oil — 3 tbsp / 45 ml
Sesame seeds (*til*) — 2 tsp / 4 gm
Cumin (*jeera*) seeds — 2 tsp / 4 gm

Asafoetida (*hing*) — a pinch

Coconut (*nariyal*), grated — 3 tbsp / 12 gm
Green coriander (*hara dhaniya*), chopped — 2 tbsp / 8 gm

Method:

1. Spread some of the prepared paste over one piece of a colocasia leaf and roll into a tight cylinder. Secure with a string. Similarly, prepare the others.
2. Steam the rolls for 5 minutes. Remove and cut each roll into slices.
3. **For the tempering**, heat the oil; add the ingredients and sauté. Add the slices and stir till well mixed.
4. Serve garnished with coconut and green coriander.

Surati Patties

Potato cakes filled with dry fruits and coconut

Preparation time: 30 min.
Cooking time: 10 min.
Serves: 6-8

Ingredients:

Potatoes, boiled, mashed till smooth   500 gm
Salt to taste
Refined flour (*maida*)   2 tbsp / 20 gm
For the filling, mix well together:
Coconut (*nariyal*), fresh, grated 1 cup / 100 gm
Green coriander (*hara dhaniya*),
   finely chopped   2 cups / 50 gm
Green chillies, finely chopped   2
Garlic (*lasan*), chopped (optional) 2 tsp / 6 gm
Cashew nuts (*kaju*), chopped   1 tbsp / 15 gm
Raisins (*kishmish*)   1 tbsp / 10 gm
Sugar   1 tbsp / 20 gm
Salt to taste

Vegetable oil for deep-frying

Method:

1. Add salt and flour to the potatoes. Knead into a soft dough.

2. Grease your palms, take a small amount of the potato mixture and shape into a flat, round cake.

3. Put about 2 tsp of the filling in the centre, roll into a round ball, ensuring that the filling stays in. Flatten into a small, round cake. Similarly, prepare the other cakes.

4. Heat the oil in a wok (*kadhai*); deep-fry the cakes on a high flame till golden brown. Remove with a slotted spoon and drain the excess oil on absorbent kitchen towels.

5. Serve with *kothmir ni chutney* (see p. 82).

Methi Na Thepla
Thin chapatis flavoured with fenugreek

Preparation time: 10 min.
Cooking time: 15 min.
Serves: 4-5

Ingredients:

Fenugreek (*methi*) leaves, finely chopped	1 cup / 30 gm
Wholewheat flour (*atta*)	2 cups / 200 gm
Vegetable oil	3 tbsp / 45 ml
Cumin (*jeera*) powder	½ tsp / ¾ gm
Coriander (*dhaniya*) powder	½ tsp / ¾ gm
Turmeric (*haldi*) powder	½ tsp / 1 gm
Red chilli powder	1 tsp / 2 gm
Salt to taste	
Vegetable oil for shallow frying	

Method:

1. Mix the fenugreek leaves with the wholewheat flour. Add all the other ingredients (except oil for frying), knead with just enough water to make a medium-soft dough.
2. Divide the dough equally into small, round balls. Roll out each ball into a very thin disc.
3. Heat a griddle (*tawa*) on high heat; lower heat, lay a disc flat over it and cook on both sides till small bubbles appear on the surface.
4. Increase the flame to medium; sprinkle ½ tbsp oil around and ¼ tbsp oil over the disc. Fry on both sides till small brown spots appear. Remove and repeat with the other discs.
5. Serve warm or cold at teatime.

Methi Na Dhebra

Millet flour chapatis flavoured with fenugreek

Preparation time: 20 min.
Cooking time: 15 min.
Serves: 4-5

Ingredients:

Fenugreek leaves (*methi*), chopped	2 cups / 60 gm
Millet flour (*bajre ka atta*)	1 cup / 100 gm
Wholewheat flour (*atta*)	¼ cup / 25 gm
Gram flour (*besan*)	1 tbsp / 10 gm
Red chilli powder	½ tsp / 1 gm
Asafoetida (*hing*)	¼ tsp / 1 gm
Semolina (*suji*)	¼ tsp
Yoghurt (*dahi*), fresh	½ cup / 90 gm
Garlic (*lasan*), fresh, chopped	1 tbsp / 12 gm
Green chillies, small, chopped	3
Vegetable oil	1 tbsp / 15 ml
Sugar	1 tsp / 3 gm
Salt to taste	
Vegetable oil for shallow frying	

Method:

1. Mix all the ingredients (except the oil) and knead with just enough water to make a soft dough.
2. Divide the dough equally into small balls. Roll each ball out into a 4" disc.
3. Heat a griddle (*tawa*) on high heat. Lower heat to minimum and lay a disc flat over it; cook on both sides till small bubbles appear on the surface. Increase the flame to medium; sprinkle ½ tbsp oil around the disc and ¼ tbsp oil on the surface of the disc. Fry till small brown spots appear on both sides. Remove from the griddle at once.
4. Repeat till all the discs are ready.
5. Serve warm or cold at teatime.

Chewdo

Spicy snack made of beaten rice and dry fruits

Preparation time: 15 min.
Cooking time: 15 min.
Serves: 6-8

Ingredients:

Beaten rice (*chewda*)	5 cups / 250 gm
Vegetable oil for frying	
Cashew nuts (*kaju*)	2 tbsp / 30 gm
Dry coconut (*copra*), sliced	¼
Curry leaves (*kadhi patta*)	10-12
Green chilli	1
Peanuts (*moongphalli*)	¼ cup / 50 gm
Raisins (*kishmish*)	2 tbsp / 20 gm
Sugar	½ tsp / 1½ tsp
Turmeric powder (*haldi*)	½ tsp / 1 gm
Red chilli powder	1 tsp / 2 gm
Salt to taste	

Method:

1. Heat the oil in a wok (*kadhai*); fry each of the following: cashew nuts till light brown, dry coconut till golden, raisins till light brown, green chillies and curry leaves till slightly wilted, and peanuts till pale golden.

2. Heat the oil to smoking point; deep-fry the beaten rice till they puff up. Remove with a slotted spoon and drain the excess oil.

3. Mix in the turmeric powder, red chilli powder, peanuts, cashew nuts, coconut, green chilli, raisins, and curry leaves. Add salt only when the mixture has cooled down.

4. Store in an airtight jar.

Kobi Na Moothia
Delicious steamed cabbage dumplings

Preparation time: 15 min.
Cooking time: 25 min.
Serves: 4-6

Ingredients:

Cabbage (*bandh gobi*), finely shredded	250 gm
Salt to taste	
Gram flour (*besan*)	1 cup / 100 gm
Asafoetida (*hing*) powder	¼ tsp / 1 gm
Green chillies	3
Ginger (*adrak*) paste	1 tsp / 6 gm
Bicarbonate of soda	¼ tsp / 1½ gm
Lemon (*nimbu*) juice	1
Sugar	1 tbsp / 20 gm
Vegetable oil	2 tbsp / 30 ml

For the tempering:

Vegetable oil	1 tbsp / 15 ml
Mustard seeds (*rai*)	½ tsp / 1½ gm
Cumin (*jeera*) seeds	½ tsp / 1 gm
Red chilli powder	1 tsp / 2 gm
Curry leaves (*kadhi patta*)	10
Turmeric (*haldi*) powder	½ tsp / 1 gm
Asafoetida (*hing*)	a pinch

Method:

1. Mix the salt with the cabbage; keep aside for 20 minutes. Squeeze out the juice from the cabbage.
2. Add the gram flour, and the other ingredients. Knead with enough water to make a soft dough.
3. With wet palms, make sausage-shape rolls; about ½-¾″ diameter. Steam the rolls for 15-20 minutes in a steamer. Remove, cool and cut into ½″ pieces.
4. **For the tempering**, heat the oil; add the mustard seeds; sauté. Add the remaining ingredients and the steamed rolls; sauté for 5 minutes and serve.

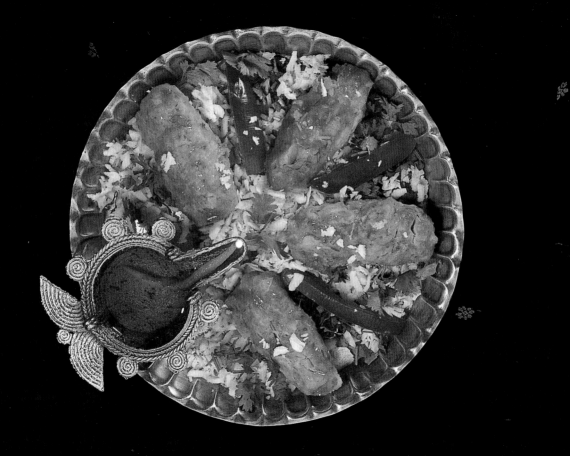

Beans Nu Shak

Beans cooked in Surati style

Preparation time: 5 min.
Cooking time: 15 min.
Serves: 2

Dry Dishes

Ingredients:

French beans, finely chopped	250 gm
Vegetable oil	2 tsp / 10 ml
Water	1 cup / 200 ml
Asafoetida (*hing*)	a pinch
Carom seeds (*ajwain*)	¼ tsp
Sugar	½ tsp / 1½ gm
or	
Jaggery (*gur*)	1½ tsp / 15 gm
Green chillies, slit lengthwise	2
Green coriander (*hara dhaniya*), chopped	½ tbsp / 2 gm

Method:

1. Add 1 tsp oil in the water. Keep aside.
2. Heat the remaining oil in a pan; add the asafoetida and sauté for a few seconds. Add the French beans, the water-oil mixture and the carom seeds. Cook uncovered, on a medium flame, for about 5 minutes or till the beans are tender.
3. Add sugar or jaggery, green chillies, and green coriander. Mix and serve hot.

Note: *Always ensure that the beans are fresh and tender otherwise you will not enjoy this dish. Vegetables taste best when served immediately.*

Sambhariya Kaddu

Sweet and sour red pumpkin

Preparation time: 10 min.
Cooking time: 20 min.
Serves: 4-6

Dry Dishes

Ingredients:

Red pumpkin (*lal kaddu*), cut into ½" cubes	500 gm
Ghee	1 tbsp / 15 gm
Bay leaf (*tej patta*)	1
Cumin (*jeera*) seeds	½ tsp / 1 gm
Coriander (*dhaniya*) seeds	½ tsp / 1 gm
Fenugreek seeds (*methi dana*)	½ tsp / 1½ gm
Fennel (*moti saunf*), powdered	½ tsp / 1 gm
Asafoetida (*hing*)	a small pinch
Ginger (*adrak*) paste	½ tsp / 3 gm
Turmeric (*haldi*) powder	½ tsp / 1 gm
Dry red chillies (*sookhi lal mirch*)	2
Salt to taste	
Garam masala	½ tsp / 1 gm
Sugar to taste or jaggery (*gur*)	a small lump
Tamarind (*imli*)	2 tbsp / 12 gm

Method:

1. Heat the ghee in a wok (*kadhai*); add the bay leaf, cumin seeds, coriander seeds, fenugreek seeds, fennel powder, and asafoetida; sauté for a minute.
2. Add the ginger paste and red pumpkin; stir-fry for 2 minutes.
3. Add the turmeric powder, dry red chillies, and salt; stir-fry for a few minutes.
4. Add the garam masala, and cook covered till the pumpkin is half done. Add the sugar or jaggery and tamarind. Mix well, cook covered on a low flame for 15 minutes or till done. Serve with *puri*.

Tori Nu Shak

Snake gourd cooked in Surati style

Preparation time: 10 min.
Cooking time: 25 min.
Serves: 4

Dry Dishes

Ingredients:

Snake gourd (*tori*), cut into 1" cubes	500 gm
Ghee	½ tbsp / 7½ gm
Cumin (*jeera*) seeds, ground	½ tsp / 1 gm
Coconut (*nariyal*) milk (optional)	½ cup / 100 ml
Ginger (*adrak*) paste	1 tsp / 6 gm
Garlic (*lasan*) paste	1 tsp / 6 gm
Green chillies, ground to a paste	2
Green coriander (*hara dhaniya*), chopped	1 tbsp / 4 gm

Method:

1. Heat the ghee in a pan; add the cumin seeds. When they start spluttering, add the snake gourd and sauté for 5 minutes.

2. Add the coconut milk, ginger, garlic, and green chilli pastes. Cover and simmer till done.

3. Serve hot garnished with green coriander.

Valore Moothia Nu Shak

Broad beans and gram flour dumplings

Preparation time: 15 min.
Cooking time: 25 min.
Serves: 2-4

Ingredients:

Broad beans, finely chopped	300 gm
For the dough:	
Gram flour *(besan)*	1 cup / 100 gm
Red chilli powder to taste	
Fenugreek *(methi)* leaves, finely chopped	½ cup / 15 gm
Turmeric *(haldi)* powder	¼ tsp / ½ gm
Asafoetida *(hing)*	a pinch
Bicarbonate of soda	a pinch
Cumin *(jeera)* seeds, powdered	½ tsp / ¾ gm
Coriander *(dhaniya)* powder	½ tsp / ¾ gm
Salt to taste	
Vegetable oil	3½ tbsp / 52 ml
Salt to taste	

Carom seeds *(ajwain)*	1 tsp / 1½ gm
Cumin *(jeera)* seeds	1 tsp / 2 gm
Bicarbonate of soda	a pinch
Turmeric *(haldi)* powder	¼ tsp / ½ gm
Red chilli powder	½ tsp / 1 gm
Cumin *(jeera)* powder	1 tsp / 1½ gm
Coriander *(dhaniya)* powder	½ tsp / ¾ gm

Method:

1. **For the dough**, put the gram flour in a large, flat vessel in a heap. Make a well in the centre of the heap, add all the ingredients for the dough and mix well.

2. Knead with just enough water to make a soft dough. Keep aside.

3. Heat the oil in a pan; add the broad beans, salt, carom seeds, cumin seeds, and bicarbonate of soda; sauté for a while. Add ½ cup water and cook covered for 7 minutes. Add the turmeric powder, red chilli powder, cumin powder, and coriander powder. Mix well. Cook till the mixture is absolutely dry. Adjust seasoning to taste.

4. Mix this broad bean mixture with the gram flour dough and knead again.

5. With wet hands, take a small portion of the dough and shape into a small, round dumpling. Repeat till all the dough is used up. Arrange the dumplings in a big pan, ensuring that they do not overlap. Cook covered with a lid containing a little water, to help form steam for about 7 minutes.

6. Carefully remove the lid and move the dumplings around once.

7. Once the oil separates and the water evaporates, the dumplings are ready to be served.

Karela Bhindu Nu Shak

Okra and bitter gourd flavoured with asafoetida

Preparation time: 1 hr.
Cooking time: 20 min.
Serves: 2

Ingredients:

Okra (*bhindi*), washed, wiped dry,
   cut into pieces   250 gm
Bitter gourd (*karela*),
   cut into thin round slices   150 gm
Vegetable oil   2 tbsp / 30 ml
Asafoetida (*hing*)   a pinch
Turmeric (*haldi*) powder   ¼ tsp / ½ gm
Red chilli powder   ½ tsp / 1 gm
Cumin (*jeera*) powder   ½ tsp / ¾ gm
Coriander (*dhaniya*) powder   1 tsp / 1½ gm
Sugar   1 tsp / 3 gm
Salt to taste

Method:

1. Mix 2 tsp salt with the bitter gourd and keep aside for 1 hour. Squeeze out the liquid from the bitter gourd.

2. Heat the oil in a pan; add the asafoetida, okra, and bitter gourd. Sauté over a medium flame for 10 minutes.

3. When cooked, add the turmeric powder, red chilli powder, cumin powder, coriander powder, sugar, and salt. Cook for about 5 minutes more and serve with *roti* or *methi na thepla* (see p. 26).

43

Sambhariya Bhindi

Stuffed okra cooked in yoghurt

Preparation time: 10 min.
Cooking time: 10 min.
Serves: 2

Dry Dishes

Ingredients:

Okra (*bhindi*), slit lengthwise	250 gm
Vegetable oil for frying	
Yoghurt (*dahi*), whisked	2 tbsp / 60 gm
Salt to taste	

For the filling:

Coconut (*nariyal*), grated	2 tbsp / 8 gm
Green chilli paste	½ tsp / 2½ gm
Green coriander (*hara dhaniya*)	½ cup / 12½ gm
Cumin-coriander (*jeera-dhaniya*) powder	½ tsp / ¾ gm
Ginger (*adrak*) paste	¼ tsp / 1½ gm

Method:

1. **For the filling**, mix all the ingredients together. Carefully stuff each okra with this filling.

2. Heat the oil in a frying pan till smoking; lower the flame to medium, deep-fry the stuffed okra, a few at a time, until soft. Remove with a slotted spoon, drain the excess oil on absorbent kitchen towels.

3. In a separate pan, add the yoghurt and the fried okra; cook on a low flame for approximately 3-4 minutes. Do not bring the mixture to the boil or else the yoghurt will curdle. Add salt to taste and mix well.

4. Serve hot.

Surati Baingan Aloo Nu Shak

A potato and aubergine preparation

Preparation time: 10 min.
Cooking time: 25 min.
Serves: 4

Ingredients:

Aubergines (*baingan*), chopped	250 gm
Potatoes, chopped	250 gm
Vegetable oil	3 tbsp / 45 ml
Asafoetida (*hing*)	½ tsp / 2½ gm
Mustard seeds (*rai*)	1 tsp / 3 gm
Tomatoes, medium, finely chopped	1
Ginger-garlic (*adrak-lasan*) paste	1 tsp / 6 gm
Red chilli powder	1 tsp / 2 gm
Turmeric (*haldi*) powder	½ tsp / 1 gm
Coriander (*dhaniya*) powder	3 tsp / 4½ gm
Salt to taste	
Sugar	3 tsp / 9 gm
Water, hot	½ cup / 100 ml
Green coriander (*hara dhaniya*), chopped	1 tbsp / 4 gm

Method:

1. Heat the oil in a pan; add the asafoetida and mustard seeds. When the seeds splutter, add the tomatoes. Cook for 2 minutes, then mix in the ginger-garlic paste, red chilli powder, turmeric powder, coriander powder, salt, and sugar.

2. Add the aubergines and potatoes, mix well. Add the hot water and cook covered on a low flame for about 20 minutes or till the vegetables are done and the mixture is dry. You can also cook in a pressure cooker for 10 minutes.

3. Garnish with green coriander and serve with any salad and chutney of your choice.

Methi Moothia

Steamed fenugreek dumplings in a thick gravy

Preparation time: 10 min.
Cooking time: 25 min.
Serves: 2-4

Ingredients:

Gram flour (*besan*)	1 cup / 100 gm
Fenugreek leaves (*methi*), finely chopped	½ cup / 15 gm
Green chilli, finely chopped	1
Vegetable oil	1 tbsp / 15 ml
For the gravy:	
Vegetable oil	1 tbsp / 15 ml
Onion, medium	1
Tomatoes, peeled	2
Cumin (*jeera*) seeds	½ tsp / 1 gm
Ginger (*adrak*) paste	1 tsp / 6 gm
Garlic (*lasan*) paste	1 tsp / 6 gm

Method:

1. Sift the gram flour in a bowl, add the fenugreek leaves, green chilli and oil. Knead into a semi-hard dough and let the dough rest for 5 minutes.
2. Divide the dough into ½" round balls. Grease the steamer and steam the balls for about 7-8 minutes.
3. **For the gravy**, heat the oil in a wok (*kadhai*); add the onion and fry till brown.
4. Add the tomatoes, cumin seeds, ginger paste, and garlic paste; cook for about 10 minutes or till the gravy is thick.
5. Add the steamed balls and cook for 5 minutes.
6. Serve hot with *roti*.

Kela Na Sambhariya

Raw bananas stuffed with gram flour

Preparation time: 15 min.
Cooking time: 20 min.
Serves: 6

Dry Dishes

Ingredients:

Bananas, ends chopped	8
For the filling:	
Gram flour (*besan*)	1¼ cups / 125 gm
Turmeric (*haldi*) powder	½ tsp / 1 gm
Red chilli powder	1 tsp / 2 gm
Cumin (*jeera*) powder	1 tsp / 1½ gm
Coriander (*dhaniya*) powder	1 tsp / 1½ gm
Green chillies, chopped	4
Sugar	2 tsp / 6 gm
Salt to taste	
Vegetable oil	1 cup / 200 ml

Method:

1. Leaving the skin intact, slice the banana lengthwise, into 4 sections, just stopping short of the base.
2. **For the filling**, mix all the ingredients together.
3. Stuff the filling into the banana slices. Keep aside 2 tsp of the filling.
4. Heat the oil in a pan; place the stuffed bananas side by side. Cook on a low flame, covered with a lid containing some water, to prevent the bananas from sticking to the bottom of the pan.
5. After 10 minutes, add the remaining stuffing. Cover the pan with the lid again.
6. Stir once after 5 minutes and then remove the pan from the heat. Serve piping hot.

Vatana Bateta No Rotlo

Baked potatoes and peas

Preparation time: 30 min.
Cooking time: 25 min.
Serves: 2-4

Ingredients:

Potatoes, boiled	300 gm
Green peas (*matar*), boiled	1 cup
Rice flour	1 cup / 115 gm
Juice of lemon (*nimbu*)	1
Green chilli-ginger (*adrak*) paste	2 tbsp / 30 gm
Sugar	½ tsp / 1½ gm
Salt to taste	
Vegetable oil to grease the baking tray	

Method:

1. Lightly mash the boiled peas with your hands and keep aside.
2. Mash the potatoes in a bowl, add the peas, rice flour, lemon juice, green chilli-ginger paste, sugar, and salt; mix well.
3. Grease an 8" x 8" baking tray with a little oil.
4. Press the mixture into the baking tray and bake in a preheated oven at 200°C for 20-25 minutes or till golden and crisp.
5. Cut into squares and serve with yoghurt and chutney of your choice.

Surati Dal

Red gram cooked with tomatoes and peanuts

Preparation time: 5 min.
Cooking time: 25 min.
Serves: 3-4

Curry Dishes

Ingredients:

Split red gram (*arhar dal*)	¾ cup / 100 gm
Tomatoes, medium, grated	2
Peanuts (*moongphalli*), unroasted, with skin removed	8-10
Green chillies	2
Jaggery (*gur*)	1 tbsp / 20 gm
Curry leaves (*kadhi patta*)	6-8
Turmeric (*haldi*) powder	½ tsp / 1 gm
Red chilli powder	½ tsp / 1 gm
Salt to taste	
Ghee	2 tsp / 10 gm
Mustard seeds (*rai*)	1 tsp / 3 gm
Asafoetida (*hing*)	a pinch
Juice of lemon (*nimbu*)	1
Green coriander (*hara dhaniya*), for garnish	

Method:

1. Boil the split red gram and the tomatoes in 2½ cups water for 15 minutes or till soft. Stir constantly till a smooth consistency is obtained.

2. Add the peanuts, green chillies, jaggery, curry leaves, turmeric powder, red chilli powder, and salt. Bring the mixture to the boil.

3. Heat the ghee in a small pan; add the mustard seeds; when they splutter, add the asafoetida. Remove from the flame and add this tempering to the cooked split red gram. Bring the mixture to the boil again; mix in the lemon juice.

4. Serve hot garnished with green coriander.

Meethi Dal
Sweet and tangy split red gram

Preparation time: I hr.
Cooking time: 25 min.
Serves: 3-4

Ingredients:

Split red gram (*arhar dal*),
   soaked for 1 hour — 1 cup / 160 gm
Water — 3 cups / 600 ml

For the tempering:
Ghee — 2 tbsp / 30 gm
Mustard seeds (*rai*) — ½ tsp / 1½ gm
Cumin (*jeera*) seeds — 1 tsp / 2 gm
Fenugreek seeds (*methi dana*) — ½ tsp / 1½ gm
Asafoetida (*hing*) — a pinch
Peanuts (*moongphalli*),
   unroasted, with skin removed — 12
Curry leaves (*kadhi patta*) — 15

Jaggery (*gur*) — 1 tbsp / 20 gm
Juice of lemon (*nimbu*) — 1

Cocum or Tamarind (*imli*) extract — 3 pcs / 1 tbsp
Turmeric (*haldi*) powder — ½ tsp / 1 gm
Red chilli powder — ½ tsp / 1 gm
Coriander-cumin (*dhaniya-jeera*) powder — 1 tsp / 1½ gm
Salt to taste

Method:

1. Pressure cook the split red gram in 2 cups water till 3 whistles. Release the pressure and open the lid carefully. Whip until thick; mix in 1 cup water.

2. **For the tempering**, heat the ghee in a pan; sauté the tempering ingredients for a few seconds, and pour over the boiled red gram.

3. Add the remaining ingredients and cook covered for 10 minutes on a medium flame. Serve hot.

Meethi Kadhi
Sweet yoghurt curry

Preparation time: 5 min.
Cooking time: 20 min.
Serves: 6-8

Ingredients:

Yoghurt (*dahi*), sour   2 cups / 360 gm
Gram flour (*besan*)   2 tbsp / 20 gm
Ginger (*adrak*), 1" piece, finely chopped   1
Jaggery (*gur*)   2 tbsp / 40 gm
Green coriander (*hara dhaniya*),
    chopped   ½ cup / 12 gm
Curry leaves (*kadhi patta*)   2-3 sprigs
Salt to taste
For the tempering:
Vegetable oil   1 tsp / 5 ml
Cumin (*jeera*) seeds   ½ tsp / 1 gm
Fenugreek seeds (*methi dana*)   ¼ tsp / ¾ gm
Cloves (*laung*)   2-3
Cinnamon (*dalchini*), 1" stick   1
Asafoetida (*hing*)   ¼ tsp / 1 gm

Method:

1. Whip the yoghurt, adding enough water to obtain a pouring consistency.
2. Add the gram flour, ginger, jaggery, green coriander, curry leaves, and salt to taste.
3. Cook on a high flame and stir constantly for about 15 minutes. The mixture should not be too sweet.
4. **For the tempering,** heat the oil in a pan; add the cumin seeds, fenugreek seeds, cloves, cinnamon stick, and asafoetida; sauté for a few seconds. Pour the yoghurt mixture and simmer for 2 minutes. Adjust seasoning to taste.
5. Serve hot with any vegetable.

Surati Kadhi

Spicy yoghurt and gram flour curry

Preparation time: 10 min.
Cooking time: 15-20 min.
Serves: 4-5

Ingredients:

Yoghurt (*dahi*)	1½ cup / 270 gm
Gram flour (*besan*)	2 tbsp / 20 gm
Water	1 cup / 200 ml
Green chilli-ginger (*adrak*) paste	1 tsp / 6 gm
Sugar	2 tbsp / 40 gm
Curry leaves (*kadhi patta*)	6-8
Ghee	1 tsp / 5 gm
Cumin (*jeera*) powder	1 tsp / 1½ gm
Green coriander (*hara dhaniya*), chopped	1 tbsp / 4 gm

Method:

1. Whisk the yoghurt and gram flour together into a creamy consistency, gradually adding water.
2. Add all the ingredients except the ghee and cumin powder. Bring the mixture to the boil, stirring constantly.
3. Heat the ghee in a wok (*kadhai*); add the cumin powder, fry for a few seconds and add to the yoghurt mixture.
4. Garnish with green coriander and serve hot with steamed rice.

Sambhariya Ringanani Kadhi

Fried aubergines in a spicy yoghurt curry

Preparation time: 30 min.
Cooking time: 30 min.
Serves: 4-6

Ingredients:

Aubergines (*baingan*), small, round, cut lengthwise, soaked in saline water for ½ hour	9-10
Yoghurt (*dahi*)	½ cup / 90 gm
Ginger-garlic (*adrak-lasan*) paste	2 tsp / 12 gm
Garam masala	1 tsp / 2 gm
Cumin-coriander (*jeera-dhaniya*) powder	1 tsp / 1½ gm
Red chilli powder	1 tsp / 2 gm
Ghee	2 tsp / 10 gm

For the gravy:

Cinnamon (*dalchini*), 1" sticks	2
Cumin (*jeera*) seeds	¼ tsp / ½ gm
Coconut (*nariyal*), grated	2 tsp / 4 gm
Green coriander (*hara dhaniya*)	1 cup / 25 gm
Coriander (*dhaniya*) powder	1 tsp / 1½ gm
Poppy seeds (*khuskhus*)	1 tsp / 2 gm
Green chilli-ginger (*adrak*) paste	1 tbsp / 15 gm
Garlic (*lasan*) cloves	8
Salt to taste	
Black peppercorns (*sabut kali mirch*)	8-10
Ghee	3 tbsp / 45 gm
Onion, medium, grated	1
Turmeric (*haldi*) powder	½ tsp / 1 gm
Green peas (*matar*), shelled, boiled	1 cup

Method:

1. Mix the yoghurt with the ginger-garlic paste, garam masala, cumin-coriander powder, and red chilli powder.

2. Heat the ghee in a shallow pan; sauté the aubergines, turning frequently. Cook covered on a low flame for about 15 minutes. Keep aside.

3. **For the gravy**, grind together all the ingredients (except the last 4).

4. In a separate pan, heat the ghee; sauté the onion till golden brown. Add the ground ingredients and sauté for 5 minutes over a medium flame until the oil separates. If the mixture starts to stick to the bottom of the pan, sprinkle some water.

5. Add the turmeric powder and yoghurt mixture, mix well. Add the green peas and stir. Bring the mixture to the boil and adjust seasoning.

6. Add the fried aubergines and bring to the boil again. Cover and simmer for 5 minutes.

7. Serve hot garnished with green coriander.

Note: *All Gujarati meals are served with ghee, though the quantity used while cooking is nominal. Ghee lends a distinct and interesting flavour to the food.*

⁀

Selecting Aubergines
Buy aubergines which are heavy, firm, free from blemish and of a uniform dark colour.

⁀

Khatta Mag

Sweet and sour green gram

Preparation time: 1 hr.
Cooking time: 20 min.
Serves: 5-6

Ingredients:

Whole green gram (*moong dal*), soaked in
   warm water for 1 hour   1½ cups / 200 gm
Yoghurt (*dahi*)   1 cup / 180 gm
Green chillies, ground   2
Ginger (*adrak*), 1" piece, ground   1
Turmeric (*haldi*) powder   ½ tsp / 1 gm
Red chilli powder   1 tsp / 2 gm
Cumin-coriander (*jeera-dhaniya*) powder   1 tsp
Jaggery (*gur*)   ½ tsp / 5 gm
Salt to taste

For the tempering:
Vegetable oil   1 tbsp / 15 ml
Mustard seeds (*rai*)   ½ tsp / 1½ gm
Cumin (*jeera*) seeds   ½ tsp / 1 gm
Asafoetida (*hing*)   ¼ tsp / 1 gm

Method:

1. Add 3 cups water to the whole green gram and pressure cook for 10 minutes or until it is well cooked. Remove from the flame and whisk till it is well mixed and smooth.

2. Reheat the green gram and add yoghurt, green chillies, ginger, turmeric powder, red chilli powder, cumin-coriander powder, jaggery, and salt. Simmer for 10 minutes.

3. **For the tempering,** heat the oil in a pan; add the mustard seeds. When they start crackling, add cumin seeds and asafoetida.

4. Mix in the green gram mixture, and adjust seasoning. Simmer for 5 minutes and serve hot.

Mag Na Dal Na Khichdi

Green gram cooked with rice

Preparation time: 30 min.
Cooking time: 15 min.
Serves: 5-6

Ingredients:

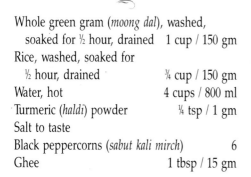

Whole green gram (*moong dal*), washed,
   soaked for ½ hour, drained   1 cup / 150 gm
Rice, washed, soaked for
   ½ hour, drained   ¾ cup / 150 gm
Water, hot   4 cups / 800 ml
Turmeric (*haldi*) powder   ¼ tsp / 1 gm
Salt to taste
Black peppercorns (*sabut kali mirch*)   6
Ghee   1 tbsp / 15 gm

Method:

1. Cook the green gram and rice in a pressure cooker. Add the water, turmeric powder, salt, and black peppercorns.

2. Allow one whistle, wait for the pressure in the cooker to subside and then open the cooker carefully. Add ghee, adjust seasoning and serve. It should be of pouring consistency.

Shak Vala Bhat

Mixed vegetable pulao

Preparation time: 1 hr.
Cooking time: 30 min.
Serves: 6-8

Accompaniments

Ingredients:

Rice, Basmati, soaked for 1 hour, drained	2 cups / 400 gm
Vegetable oil	3 tbsp / 45 ml
Cloves (*laung*)	6
Cinnamon (*dalchini*), 1" stick	1
Black peppercorns (*sabut kali mirch*)	1 tsp
Water, hot	4 cups / 800 ml
Green peas (*matar*), shelled	50 gm
Potatoes, peeled, cut into 1" cubes	250 gm
Carrots (*gajar*), peeled, cut into 1" cubes	100 gm
Turmeric (*haldi*) powder	¼ tsp / ½ gm
Green chillies, cut into 1" pieces	3
Salt to taste	
Lemon (*nimbu*) juice	1

Method:

1. Heat the oil in a pan; add the cloves, cinnamon stick, and black peppercorns. When they crackle, add the rice and sauté over a low flame for about 5 minutes.
2. Add the hot water, all the vegetables, turmeric powder, green chillies, salt, and lemon juice.
3. Cook covered for 20 minutes or till the vegetables are tender.
4. Serve hot.

Khichu

A simple Gujarati dish made of rice flour

Preparation time: 10 min.
Cooking time: 20 min.
Serves: 2-3

Ingredients:

Rice flour	1 cup / 115 gm
Water	1½ cups / 300 ml
Cumin (*jeera*) seeds	½ tsp / 1 gm
Red chilli powder	¼ tsp / ½ gm
Asafoetida (*hing*)	¼ tsp / 1 gm
Green chillies, chopped	½ tsp
Salt to taste	
Bicarbonate of soda	¼ tsp / 1½ gm
Vegetable oil	2 tbsp / 30 ml
Green coriander (*hara dhaniya*), chopped	1 tbsp / 4 gm

Method:

1. Boil the water in a pan. Add the cumin seeds, red chilli powder, asafoetida, green chillies, and salt. Mix well.
2. Add the rice flour and bicarbonate of soda, stir vigorously with a wooden spoon to avoid lumps. Cover and simmer for 10-12 minutes.
3. Add the oil and green coriander. Mix well.
4. Serve hot with ghee, crushed *pappad*, pickle and yoghurt.

Vatanano Pulao
Peas pulao garnished with fried onions

Preparation time: 1 hr.
Cooking time: 20 min.
Serves: 5-6

Ingredients:

Rice, Basmati, soaked for 1 hour	2½ cups / 500 gm
Vegetable oil	2½ tsp / 12 ml
Onion, large, sliced	1
Green cardamoms (*choti elaichi*)	5
Cloves (*laung*)	7-8
Bay leaf (*tej patta*)	1
Cinnamon (*dalchini*), 1″ stick	1
Green peas (*matar*), shelled	500 gm
Water, hot	5 cups / 1 lt
Salt to taste	
Onion, sliced, fried	1

Method:

1. Heat the oil in a pan; add the onion and fry till golden brown. Remove with a slotted spoon and drain the excess oil on absorbent kitchen towels.

2. In the same oil, add the green cardamoms, cloves, bay leaf, and cinnamon stick. Sauté for a few seconds. Add the rice and stir-fry for 4 minutes on a medium flame.

3. Add the peas and sauté for another 3 minutes. Add hot water and salt. Cook covered until the rice and peas are tender and all the water has been absorbed.

4. Serve hot garnished with fried onions.

Makkai Ni Khichdi

An interesting preparation made with corn

Preparation time: 25 min.
Cooking time: 30 min.
Serves: 2-3

Ingredients:

Corn cobs (*bhutta*), tender, grated	5
Vegetable oil	2 tbsp / 30 ml
Mustard seeds (*rai*)	½ tsp / 1½ gm
Cumin (*jeera*) seeds	½ tsp / 1 gm
Asafoetida (*hing*)	¼ tsp / 1 gm
Green chillies, chopped	2
Sugar	1 tsp / 3 gm
Salt to taste	
Juice of lemon (*nimbu*)	½
Green coriander (*hara dhaniya*), chopped	1 tbsp / 4 gm

Method:

1. Heat the oil in a pan; add the mustard seeds, cumin seeds, asafoetida, and green chillies. Sauté till the seeds crackle. Add the corn and cook on a low flame for 5 minutes.
2. Add just enough water to cover the corn. Add the sugar and salt. Cover and simmer till the corn is tender.
3. Add the lemon juice and mix well.
4. Serve hot garnished with green coriander.

Peela Bhat
Yellow rice

Preparation time: 45 min.
Cooking time: 10 min.
Serves: 4-5

Ingredients:

Rice, Basmati, washed, soaked for
    45 minutes, drained   1½ cups / 300 gm
Water   2½ cups / 500 ml
Ghee   1½ tbsp / 22 gm
Cloves (*laung*)   5
Cinnamon (*dalchini*), 1½" stick   1
Turmeric (*haldi*) powder   ¾ tsp / 1½ gm
Salt to taste

Method:

1. Bring the water to the boil.
2. Meanwhile, heat the ghee in a pressure cooker; add the cloves and cinnamon stick. Once they crackle, add the rice. Sauté for a few seconds, add the boiling water, turmeric powder, and salt.
3. Pressure cook on high heat till 2 whistles.
4. Remove the rice once the pressure subsides.
5. Serve hot accompanied with *kadhi*.

(Photograph on facing page, right)

Fada Ni Khichdi

Green gram and broken wheat with vegetables

Preparation time: 15 min.
Cooking time: 30 min.
Serves: 4-5

Ingredients:

Split green gram (*dhuli moong dal*), washed,
    soaked for 15 minutes   1 cup / 190 gm
Broken wheat (*dalia*), washed,
    soaked for 15 minutes   ¾ cup

For the tempering:
Ghee   3 tbsp / 45 gm
Cinnamon (*dalchini*), 1" stick   1
Cloves (*laung*)   3
Cumin (*jeera*) seeds   1 tsp / 2 gm
Asafoetida (*hing*)   ¼ tsp / 1 gm

Green peas (*matar*)   1 cup
Potatoes, diced   1 cup
Cauliflower (*phool gobi*), florets   1 cup
Onions, diced   1 cup

Green chilli-ginger (*adrak*) paste   1 tbsp / 15 gm
Black peppercorns (*sabut kali mirch*)   ½ tsp
Red chilli powder   1 tsp / 2 gm
Turmeric (*haldi*) powder   ½ tsp / 1 gm
Salt to taste
Water, hot   2½ cups / 500 ml

Method:

1. **For the tempering**, heat the ghee in a pressure cooker; add the cinnamon stick, cloves, cumin seeds, and asafoetida. Sauté for 30 seconds.
2. Add the green peas, potatoes, cauliflower, onions and the green chilli-ginger paste. Sauté for a few minutes, or till the vegetables are a little tender.
3. Add the drained split green gram and broken

wheat, black peppercorns, red chilli powder, turmeric powder, and salt. Stir-fry for 4-5 minutes.

4. Add the hot water and pressure cook for 3-4 whistles.

5. Allow the steam to escape, then open the pressure cooker carefully.

6. Stir vigorously, adding a little more hot water, if required, so that the split green gram and the broken wheat mix well. Adjust seasoning, if required.

7. Serve hot.

⤳

Hot Dip

To soak dal at a short notice,
use hot water instead of cold water.

⤳

Surati Saalad

Crunchy cucumber salad

Preparation time: 10 min.
Cooking time: 2 min.
Serves: 3-4

A c c o m p a n i m e n t s

Ingredients:

Cucumber (*khira*), small, diced	250 gm
Vegetable oil	1 tsp / 5 ml
Asafoetida (*hing*)	a pinch
Bengal gram (*chana dal*), roasted	1 tbsp / 25 gm
Peanuts (*moongphalli*), roasted, chopped	1 tbsp / 15 gm
Coconut (*nariyal*), fresh, grated	1 tbsp / 4 gm
Sesame seeds (*til*), roasted	1 tsp / 2 gm
Green chillies, finely chopped	2
Sugar	½ tsp / 1½ gm
Salt to taste	

Method:

1. Heat the oil in a pan; add the asafoetida and Bengal gram; sauté for 2 minutes.
2. In a large bowl, mix the peanuts, coconut, sesame seeds, green chillies, sugar, and salt together.
3. Mix in the Bengal gram-asafoetida mixture and cucumber. Adjust seasoning and serve.

Papaya Saalad
Raw papaya salad

Preparation time: 10 min.
Cooking time: 2 min.
Serves: 2-4

Ingredients:

Papaya (*papita*), raw, small, peeled, coarsely grated	250 gm
Vegetable oil	1 tsp / 5 ml
Asafoetida (*hing*)	a pinch
Mustard seeds (*rai*)	¼ tsp / ¾ gm
Green chillies, slit	4-5
Cumin (*jeera*) seeds	¼ tsp / ½ gm
Sugar	1 tsp / 3 gm
Peanuts (*moongphalli*), chopped	1 tbsp / 15 gm
Juice of lemon (*nimbu*)	1
Green coriander (*hara dhaniya*), finely chopped	1 tsp
Salt to taste	

Method:

1. Heat the oil in a pan; add the asafoetida and mustard seeds. When they start spluttering, add the green chillies; sauté.
2. Add the papaya, cumin seeds, sugar, peanuts, lemon juice, green coriander, and salt; mix thoroughly, and remove from heat. Keep aside to cool.
3. Serve cold as an accompaniment.

Fangevela Mag
Sprouted green gram salad

Preparation time: 8 hrs. + I day
Cooking time: 10 min.
Serves: 2-4

A c c o m p a n i m e n t s

Ingredients:

Whole green gram (*moong dal*), soaked for 8 hours	1²/₃ cups / 250 gm
Vegetable oil	1 tsp / 5 ml
Mustard seeds (*rai*)	½ tsp / 1½ gm
Asafoetida (*hing*)	¼ tsp / 1 gm
Water	1½ cups / 300 ml
Bicarbonate of soda	¼ tsp / 1½ gm
Salt to taste	
Sugar	½ tsp / 1½ gm
Cumin (*jeera*) powder	1 tsp / 1½ gm
Turmeric (*haldi*) powder	¼ tsp / ½ gm
Red chilli powder	¾ tsp / 1½ gm
Coriander (*dhaniya*) powder	1 tsp / 1½ gm

Method:

1. Drain the green gram and tie in a muslin cloth. Keep the cloth inside a vessel in a cool place and cover it tightly. Keep aside for 24 hours to allow the green gram to sprout.
2. Heat the oil in a pan; add the mustard seeds. Once they crackle, add the asafoetida and the sprouted green gram.
3. Add the water, bicarbonate of soda, salt, sugar, and the spices. Mix well. Cook covered for 10 minutes or until tender.
4. Serve hot with any *kadhi*.

Imli Ni Chutney

Easy-to-make tamarind chutney

Preparation time: 5 min.
Cooking time: 15 min.

Ingredients:

Tamarind (*imli*)	100 gm
Cumin (*jeera*) seeds	1 tsp / 2 gm
Asafoetida (*hing*)	a small pinch
Jaggery (*gur*)	3 tbsp / 60 gm
Salt to taste	
Black salt (*kala namak*)	a pinch
Red chilli powder to taste	

Method:

1. Boil the tamarind in 2 cups water for about 5 minutes. Then strain through a sieve. Keep aside.
2. Dry roast the cumin seeds and asafoetida. Grind to a fine powder.
3. Add the jaggery, cumin-asafoetida powder, salt, black salt, and red chilli powder to the tamarind extract.
4. Mix well and serve.

(Photograph on facing page, left)

Accompaniments

Kothmir Ni Chutney

Hot garlic, coriander and peanut chutney

Ingredients:

Garlic (*lasan*) cloves	½ cup
Peanuts (*moongphalli*), unroasted	1 cup / 200 gm
Cumin (*jeera*) seeds	2 tbsp / 16 gm
Green chillies	10
Sugar	3 tbsp / 60 gm
Juice of lemon (*nimbu*)	1
Salt to taste	
Green coriander (*hara dhaniya*), chopped	10 cups / 250 gm

Method:

1. Blend all the ingredients together except the green coriander to a smooth paste.
2. Add the green coriander and blend further into a smooth paste.
3. Store in a dry airtight jar, and refrigerate. Stays for up to 10-12 days.

(Photograph on page 81, right)

Kaachi Keri Ni Chutney

Raw mango chutney

Ingredients:

Mangoes, large, raw, peeled,
   deseeded, grated   250 gm
Cumin (*jeera*) seeds,
   roasted, powdered   1 tsp / 2 gm
Green coriander (*hara dhaniya*),
   chopped   1 cup / 25 gm
Sugar   1¼ tsp / 3¾ gm
Salt to taste

Method:

1. Grind together all the ingredients into a smooth paste, adding minimum water.
2. Adjust seasoning to taste and serve.

Mircha Nu Athanu
Green chilli pickle

Ingredients:

Green chillies, thick, washed, dried	500 gm
For the filling:	
Black salt (*kala namak*)	¾ cup
Mustard (*sarson*) powder	¾ tsp / 1½ gm
Asafoetida (*hing*)	½ tsp / 1 gm
Turmeric (*haldi*) powder	1 tsp / 2 gm
Vegetable oil	2 tbsp / 30 ml
Juice of lemons (*nimbu*)	2

Method:

1. Slit each chilli lengthwise. Gently tap the sides to remove the excess seeds.
2. **For the filling,** mix the black salt, mustard powder, asafoetida, turmeric powder, and oil together in a bowl.
3. Stuff the filling in each chilli. Put the stuffed chillies in a sterilised bottle. Top with leftover filling, if any.
4. Add the lemon juice and shake the bottle well.
5. Store for at least 1 day before serving.

Chundo
Shredded mango pickle

Ingredients:

Mangoes, raw, peeled, shredded	1½ kg
Salt	1½ tbsp
Turmeric (*haldi*) powder	1 tsp / 2 gm
Sugar	10 cups / 1½ kg
Red chilli powder	½ cup
Cumin (*jeera*) seeds, roasted, ground	3 tbsp / 18 gm

Method:

1. Mix the mangoes, salt and turmeric powder together with your hands. Keep aside for 2 hours.

2. Now add sugar, mix well; transfer the contents into a jar and keep aside for a day. Stir the mixture twice during the day.

3. Keep the jar covered with a muslin cloth, in the sun for 7 days. At night keep the jar indoor.

4. Before returning the jar to the sun in the mornings, stir once and retie the cloth.

5. On the eight day, add the red chilli powder and cumin powder. Mix well, cover the jar and return to the sun for another 2 days.

6. Store the pickle in a dry, airtight glass jar. Stir once every 15 days, for a period of 2 months.

Moong Dal Sheera

A traditional sweet made of green gram

Preparation time: 5 hrs.
Cooking time: 30 min.
Serves: 4

Desserts

Ingredients:

Split green gram (*dhuli moong dal*), soaked for 5 hours	1 cup / 190 gm
Ghee	6 tbsp / 90 gm
Milk, hot	1 cup / 180 ml
Water, warm	1 cup / 200 ml
Sugar	1 cup / 150 gm
Saffron (*kesar*), dissolved in 1 tbsp hot milk	a few strands
Green cardamom (*choti elaichi*) seeds, powdered	5
Almonds (*badam*), blanched, cut into slivers	10
Pistachios (*pista*), blanched, cut into slivers	10

Method:

1. Drain the split green gram and grind to a coarse paste using very little water. Drain the excess water which may remain after the grinding is over.
2. Heat the ghee in a wok (*kadhai*); add the split green gram paste and stir continuously on a low flame till it becomes golden brown.
3. Add the milk and warm water; cook, stirring continuously, till the mixture is absolutely dry.
4. Add the sugar and cook on a low flame till the oil separates. Add the saffron and green cardamom powder, mix well.
5. Serve hot garnished with almonds and pistachios.

Shrikhand

An exotic yoghurt dessert

Desserts

Ingredients:

Yoghurt (*dahi*), hung for
  2 hours in a muslin cloth   2¾ cup / 500 gm
Sugar, ground   ¾ cup / 112 gm
Saffron (*kesar*), soaked in
  1 tsp water, ground   a few strands
Green cardamom (*choti elaichi*)
  seeds, powdered   4
Almonds (*badam*),
  blanched, chopped   6
Pistachios (*pista*), chopped   8

Method:

1. In a large bowl, mix the yoghurt with the sugar. Add the ground saffron, half of the green cardamom powder, almonds, and pistachios. Mix well.
2. Pour in individual bowls and serve chilled garnished with the remaining green cardamom powder, dry fruits, and rose petals if desired.

Ghau Ni Raab
Wholewheat flour pudding

Preparation time: 5 min.
Cooking time: 15 min.
Serves: 4-6

Ingredients:

Wholewheat flour (*atta*)	2 cups / 200 gm
Vegetable oil	2 tbsp / 30 ml
Water, hot	3 cups / 600 ml
Jaggery (*gur*)	4 tbsp / 80 gm
Ginger powder (*sonth*)	2 tsp / 4 gm
Almonds (*badam*), blanched	12

Method:

1. Heat the oil in a pan; add the wholewheat flour. Sauté till the flour turns light brown.
2. Add hot water, jaggery, and ginger powder. Stir until the jaggery has dissolved completely. Adjust sweetness to taste.
3. Serve piping hot, garnished with almonds.

Longer Life
Dry fruits and even saffron will remain fresh for years in a fridge.

Matho

Sweetened yoghurt flavoured with saffron

Ingredients:

Yoghurt (*dahi*), hung for
  2 hours in a muslin cloth   2²/₃ cups / 500 gm
Sugar, ground   1 cup / 150 gm
Saffron (*kesar*), soaked in
  1 tsp water, crushed   a few strands
Green cardamom (*choti elaichi*)
  seeds, powdered   8-10

Method:

1. Blend the yoghurt and sugar together.
2. Transfer the yoghurt in a bowl. Add the crushed saffron and green cardamom powder. Mix well.
3. Serve with hot *puri*.

Anti Ants

To keep ants away from sugar,
put some cloves in the container.

Suggested Menus

Appetiser and Starter

Aam Ka Panna (*Raw mango appetiser*)   8

Khandvi (*Gram flour rolls*)   12

Main Course

Surati Baingan Aloo Nu Shak   46
(*A potato and aubergine preparation*)

Surati Kadhi (*Spicy yoghurt & gram flour curry*) 58

Accompaniments

Khichu
(*A simple Gujarati dish made of rice flour*)   67

Surati Saalad (*Crunchy cucumber salad*)   74

Mircha Nu Athanu (*Green chilli pickle*)   84

Dessert

Moong Dal Sheera
(*A traditional sweet made of green gram*)   86

Appetiser and Starter

Chaach (*Buttermilk tempered with mustard seeds*) 10

Methi Na Thepla
(*Thin chapatis flavoured with fenugreek*)   26

Main Course

Methi Moothia
(*Steamed fenugreek dumplings in a thick gravy*)   48

Meethi Kadhi (*Sweet yoghurt curry*)   56

Accompaniments

Peela Bhat (*Yellow rice*)   70

Papaya Saalad (*Raw papaya salad*)   76

Chundo (*Shredded mango pickle*)   85

Dessert

Shrikhand (*An exotic yoghurt dessert*)   88

Glossary of Cooking Terms

Blanch	—	To immerse vegetables or dry fruits briefly in boiling water.
Blend	—	To mix together thoroughly two or more ingredients.
Knead	—	To work a dough by hand or machine until smooth.
Purée	—	To press food through a fine sieve or blend it in a blender or food processor to a smooth, thick mixture.
Sauté	—	Fry quickly over high heat in fat or oil.
Sieve	—	To shake a dry ingredient through a sieve or flour sifter to remove lumps.
Simmer	—	To cook gently over a low flame.
Steam	—	Cook by heat or steam. Generally food to be steamed is put in a perforated container which is placed above a pan of boiling water. The food should not come into contact with the water.
Stir-fry	—	To cook over high heat with oil or ghee, stirring briskly.
Temper	—	To fry spices and flavourings in hot oil or ghee, and to pour this over the main preparation.
Whisk	—	To beat air rapidly into a mixture with an egg beater, rotary beater or electric beater.

Index

ISBN: 81-7436-197-9

© **Roli & Janssen BV 2002**
Published in India by
Roli Books in arrangement with
Roli & Janssen
M-75 Greater Kailash II (Market)
New Delhi 110 048, India
Ph: 6442271, 6462782, 6460886
Fax: (011) 6467185, E-mail: roli@vsnl.com
Website: rolibooks.com

Photographs: Sunny Singh

Printed and bound in Singapore